Opera

Nicholas John

Oxford University Press
Music Department,
Walton Street, Oxford OX2 6DP

Contents

(Opposite) Curtain up at the ▶
London Coliseum, and (inset)
two famous opera houses:
The Royal Opera House,
Covent Garden and Sydney
Opera House, Australia.

What is opera?

Opera is drama expressed through music. We know how music can add atmosphere, tension and excitement to a play. Try testing this by turning down the volume during a film on television. Unlike a film, however, opera is live entertainment—of the most complicated kind. During a performance, hundreds of people work to make the music and the action fit exactly for every second of the show. A huge number of things can go wrong!

An opera, like a play, is often divided into acts and scenes. Unlike a play, the characters do not speak their parts but sing them. The music may be continuous or it may be cut up into separate musical 'numbers' linked by spoken conversation. In the second half of this book you can see how the music and words of scenes from six famous operas make their effect in different ways.

An orchestra accompanies the singers. The most obvious difference between an ordinary theatre and an opera house is the *orchestra pit,* below and slightly in front of the stage, where the players sit. The *conductor* beats time to keep all the musicians, performers and technicians together. He stands where he can best be seen—right at the front centre of the pit on a small platform. We, the audience, can just see his head but our attention is fixed on the stage.

From the time when opera was invented, in Italy about 400 years ago, everything that happens on stage has been an essential part of the entertainment. Any book about opera must consider the production and stage design as well as music. The first part of this book is about what goes on behind the scenes in an opera house: how the performance is planned; how the singers are chosen, trained and rehearsed; who runs the stage; and how everything is organized.

Let's begin by visiting an opera house in the middle of a performance. We slip into the back of the darkened auditorium (the place where the audience sits), and look towards the stage.

1 Inside an opera house

On stage: `Aida`

On stage, we can see a hundred people in the famous Triumph scene from *Aida* (pronounced Ay-ee-dah). The opera takes place in Ancient Egypt. Trumpeters announce a magnificent procession of Ancient Egyptian soldiers who march past cheering crowds. They have just won a war against their Ethiopian neighbours. Some Ethiopians, captured in the battle, enter in chains.

The victorious Egyptian general, Radamès, asks his King to be merciful to them. The High Priest opposes this: he demands their deaths. The King decides to free all the Ethiopian captives except two—a beautiful girl, Aida, and her father. Then he offers Radamès a reward for his victory—marriage to his daughter, a proud and jealous princess. She loves Radamès but Radamès loves the Ethiopian slave, Aida (and she loves him). Each character sings very different thoughts. The Ethiopians beg for mercy; the crowd praises the King's generosity. Radamès and Aida are desperately miserable; the princess gloats with delight; the Priests foretell disaster; Aida's father promises revenge; the King declares the Ethiopians shall go free.

▲ The famous Triumphal March from *Aida*: trumpets announce the procession of Egyptian soldiers

The spectacle of Ancient Egypt is splendid. There are dancing girls and huge trophies from the war. The costumes are covered with what looks like gold. The sound of so many voices is very impressive. When a single voice is suddenly left alone—solo—between the choruses, we realize how exciting just singing can be. And then we wonder how all those people move about on stage without falling over one another *and* keep musically together.

Let's go back five days to see what ingredients go to make up a successful performance. How was it planned? How were the singers chosen and trained? How did they rehearse? Who runs the stage, and how is everything organized? Backstage, onstage, auditorium and 'front of house'—that's what the first part of this book is all about.

Choosing and training the singers

Theatres usually have three entrances: a main entrance at the front, a smaller side one for the cheaper seats, and a very shabby one at the back for the people who work there—the Stage Door, manned by the doorkeeper. Let's go through the grand entrance foyer, past the queues at the Box Office waiting to buy tickets. A grand staircase leads up to the level of the Dress Circle (where the most expensive seats are usually situated).

If you went up the stairs during the day-time, at each level you'd hear people singing in the theatre bars. These wouldn't be drunks, but opera-singers at **coaching sessions.** A singer learns his part (or 'role') by singing it from the music score in front of him, while a pianist (**repetiteur**) accompanies him. As well as memorizing words and notes, he tries to imagine himself into the character of the part. To learn it properly may take months or even years of work.

The repetiteurs who coach singers are skilled teachers. They point out musical mistakes (such as wrong notes, or wrong rhythms), and help the singer decide on musical **phrasing**—where to take a breath which will not interrupt the sound. Learning to breathe properly (so as to avoid wasting energy) is one of the most

Poco più animato (♩ = 76)

× = breathing space

to die _____ Migh - ty King, you are no - ble and glo - rious,
col - pir _____ Ma tu, o Re, tu si - gno - re pos - sen - te,

▲ Aida's part in the Triumph scene during the 12-part chorus; her voice is suddenly the only one singing (A-B), so it is particularly important that she phrases it correctly

difficult lessons a singer learns. In these coaching sessions, the singer repeats every note and phrase until it's ready for the **conductor**—the person in charge of the musical performance—to hear.

The biggest room (and sometimes the stage itself) is used to hear (**audition**) singers who apply to join the company. Over a thousand singers may write every year and very few (perhaps five) have voices which are suitable.

What makes an opera singer?

Firstly, he or she must have a fine voice, good health and a sound memory. In addition, he must learn how to concentrate all his energies into a performance. He does daily vocal exercises to keep his voice agile, in the same way as a sportsman trains.

▲ Coaching the leading lady for a modern opera production
The 19th-century composer Donizetti training a group of singers ▶

5

To perform in opera, you need more than the right voice: you must be able to act the part convincingly. Many great performers learn stage-craft by taking small roles at first. And, of course, they learn from real life. (The famous singer Tito Gobbi, for example, remembers how he learnt to walk like an old man on stage by copying his father's walk.)

Because opera performance is such a physical activity, many singers suffer from bad nerves—sometimes for days—before the performance. The symptoms may be very odd but very real. They may have to be pushed on stage, swearing they cannot sing, before their self-discipline takes over.

The excitement of performance also has after-effects. One successful **prima donna** (the Italian for 'leading lady') relaxes by driving cars extremely fast. Opera singers have a worse reputation than other performers for unreliability and temperament. (It's rare for this to show on stage, although two sopranos did have a fight at the King's Theatre in the Haymarket during one of Handel's operas.) There are also stories of extraordinary achievements— such as learning long and difficult roles in a few hours, or carrying on a performance despite great pain. Self-discipline and determination are essential for a singer's art; bad temper and stupid behaviour may be found in any walk of life!

Voices are as different as the bodies from which they come. They naturally stretch over about two octaves:

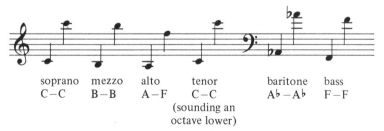

soprano   mezzo   alto   tenor   baritone   bass
C–C   B–B   A–F   C–C   A♭–A♭   F–F
                         (sounding an
                         octave lower)

but these ranges can be extended enormously by training. Boys sing treble (soprano range) or alto (mezzo range) until their voices break.

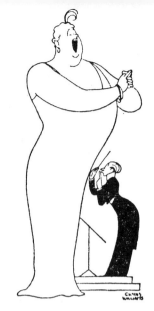

▲ Two cartoonists' views of female sopranos
▼ Luciano Pavarotti, tenor superstar, as Alfredo in Verdi's *La traviata*   ▼ Maria Callas, one of the greatest sopranos of this century, as Tosca

The management

Doors marked 'private' lead from the theatre foyers to the offices of the management. They work surrounded by piles of music scores and tape-recordings, files of letters and contracts with artists, and long address lists, sheets of telephone numbers and information about opera houses all over the world. Five or six telephones on each desk ring constantly; calendars and diaries everywhere show that planning for the next five years is in hand. Each office has a loudspeaker so that the staff can hear what is happening on stage.

An opera company is usually managed by one person (called the **Managing Director**, General Administrator, or **Intendant**); he is advised by technical, musical, administrative and financial experts. They control the different departments of the company. The Managing Director's plans depend on:

(a) people—can he hire the right singers, production team and conductor for each opera?
(b) time—is there a date convenient for all of them to prepare the production?
(c) money—can the company afford to pay them to make the production?

Planning years ahead should solve (a) and (b), and help to solve (c). Last minute alterations cost money.

Most opera houses present a 'season' during which a selection of operas from the many thousands which have been written are performed on different nights. This gives the public a choice and the artists a chance to rest between performances. The management tries to strike a balance between favourite operas (only about 50 altogether are at all well known) and less familiar ones, including new works. New operas don't always please audiences. When *Carmen*—now one of the most popular of all operas—was first performed in 1875, one of the theatre directors resigned because it ended with a murder, and the other warned the public that the new opera was 'unsuitable for unmarried girls'. Every season, some shows are new productions and the rest are *revived* ('revivals') from earlier seasons.

The press and publicity

You may hear people talking about the **reviews** of a theatre show. Journalists are invited to performances, and report on them in their newspapers. If they like the show, their comments may start a rush to buy tickets; if they don't, their bad reviews could finish an artist's career. Reviewers are often wrong: for example, two of

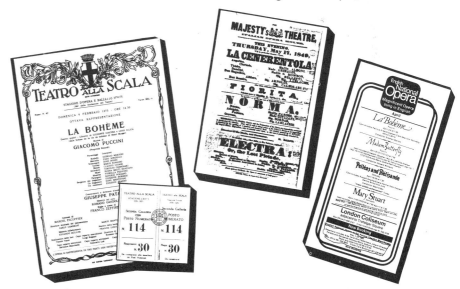

the notices of the first performance of *Carmen* (1875) said: 'there is a complete absence of light—the music dwells from start to finish in a limbo of greyness' and 'its greatest fault is that it is not dramatic'. Television and radio reach even more of the public, so their reviewers are very powerful. To keep the press informed about what is going on, and to make sure they have all the information they need, opera companies have a **press officer**.

The opera company uses newspaper adverts, leaflets and posters to announce its forthcoming shows. Nowadays, a lively publicity department is constantly thinking up other ways of keeping the opera company in the news, and of raising extra money. We can buy records, books, calendars, postcards, mugs and even T-shirts to support the company, and to advertise it.

Questions

1   Where was opera invented, and when? How is an opera different from a play?
2   Where do you normally find the Stage Door of a theatre?
3   What is an audition?
4   What are the qualities that make a good opera singer?
5   Who is a prima donna?
6   What are the jobs of these members of an opera house company: managing director, repetiteur, press officer?
7   What three considerations should you remember when planning to stage an opera?

Projects

1*a* Do some research about opera in your city/town/area. Find out the names of the buildings where opera is performed. What companies use the building and are they resident, touring, or both?
  b Is there an amateur company in your area and where do they perform? What type of people belong to it?
  c What is in the current programme at your local opera house?
  d Name three famous opera houses on the Continent. Find out some composers who worked in these houses.
2   Find out the highest and lowest notes you can sing. (Use a piano to help you find out the names of the notes.) Write them down using the chart on page 6 as a model. Then either make a chart of the vocal ranges of the members of your family (are they soprano, alto, tenor, or bass?) *or* of the people in your group.
3*a* Listen to an extract from an opera (it could be *Aida*). Can you say whether the singers you are listening to are soprano, mezzo, alto, tenor, baritone or bass?
  b Listen to recordings of different kinds of singers, for example folk, jazz, pop, and operatic. What differences do you notice in their styles of singing? Are there ways in which any of them are alike? Is it important to hear what the singers are singing about, or would you say that other things, for example melody or rhythm, were more significant?
4   Write a short review of a play, film or TV programme you've recently seen. Say what was good and bad about it, and why you think so. What was it about? Was it true to life? Was it well performed? Then, if possible, compare your review with a published review of the same performance. How does the reviewer's opinion compare with yours?
5   Interview an opera singer. If you're lucky you might be able to go backstage at your local opera house, especially if they are putting on an opera for schools. If not, then try the local music college or amateur operatic society. Ask the singer everything about his or her training, including what qualities you need to have to become an opera singer.

2 The opera house at work

The centre of an opera house is the **auditorium**. It is usually a huge hall with three, four or more balconies of seats in a horse-shoe facing the stage. The seats on the ground level are called **stalls**: between them and the stage is the **pit** where an orchestra of sometimes more than 100 players can sit. (It is sunk below the level of the stalls so that the players do not block the view of the stage.) Over 3,000 people can be seated in some opera houses.

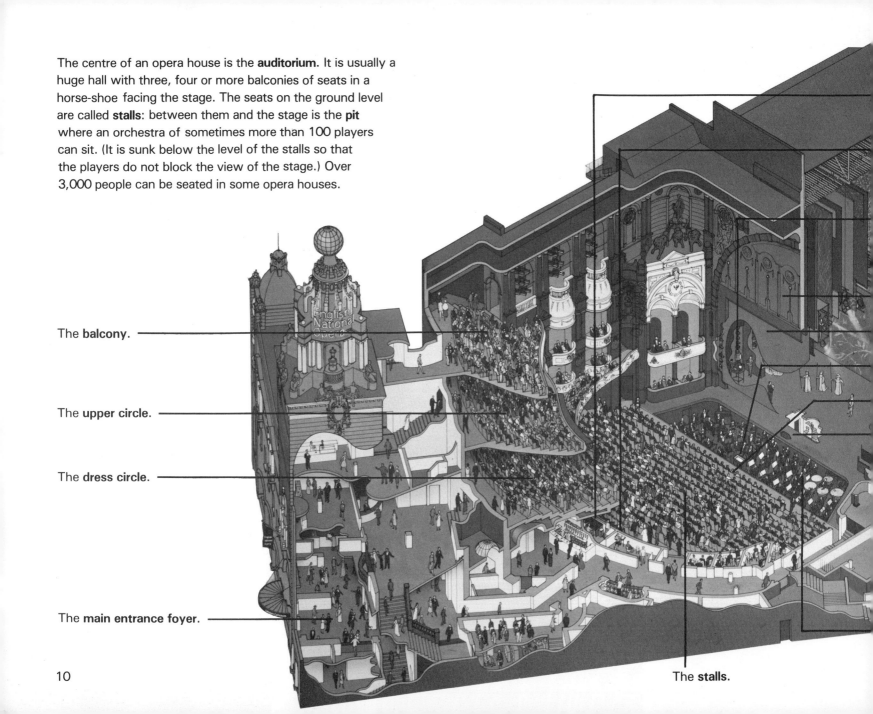

The **balcony.**

The **upper circle.**

The **dress circle.**

The **main entrance foyer.**

The **stalls.**

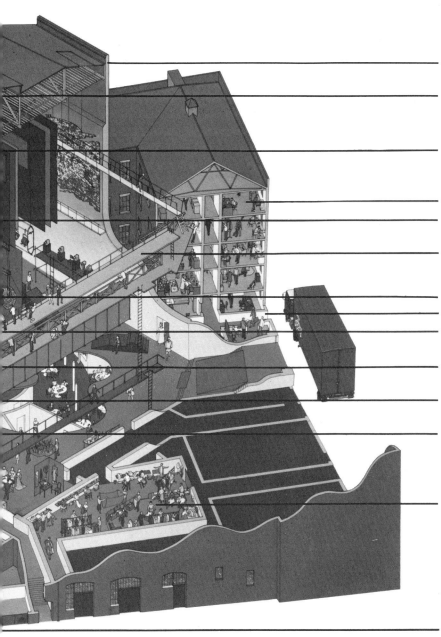

The fly tower, or the space above the stage where scenery is hung.

Lighting control box, in which a computer controlling all the lights on stage and in the auditorium is situated. It is sound-proofed and there are televisions from the pit and elsewhere.

The **production desk**, removed at the end of the rehearsal, for the production team.

The principal singers' **dressing rooms**, and offices.

The **prompt desk** where the stage manager directs the performance.

The **flies** where scenery 'flies' out of sight, operated by 'flymen'.

The velvet curtain—the **tabs**.

The **stage door**

The iron **safety curtain** to prevent a fire spreading—the 'iron' checked before each performance.

The **conductor's desk** where the conductor stands for a performance.

The **music staff desk**, removed after the rehearsal, where music staff take notes from the conductor.

The **prompt box**, in the pit, in which a member of the music staff sits during the performance on the top of a ladder, calling out the beginning of every phrase to the performers—i.e. *prompting* them.

The chorus's **dressing rooms**.

The **orchestra pit**, which goes under the stage, seats over 100 players.

A rehearsal on stage

It is a production rehearsal of the Triumph scene of *Aida* (a week before the first night performance described on page 5). It is one of the most complicated scenes in all opera because so many people have to be moved around. It is like an epic film scene. At the open air Roman arena in Verona in Italy many hundreds of performers and sometimes animals like camels and elephants take part.

At the centre of the rehearsal are the conductor (**1**), the producer and the soloists: the King, Radamès, the High Priest, Aida, the Egyptian princess and Aida's father (**2**). The special difficulty of the scene is to spotlight their private drama of love and jealousy while the huge choruses and ballets take place. So the producer sets Aida's father among the Ethiopian captives **downstage** (near the front of the stage), away from the royal Egyptians (**3**). He places the King and princess in the centre back of the stage, so that everyone else appears to be singing to them, and there is room for a ballet in front of them. When they sing themselves they can walk downstage (**4**).

Another problem is the opening chorus (**5**). It must make a huge sound: there must be a lot of people already on stage. Therefore they can't *come on* stage *later* in the procession. So he has stood them in huge ramps filling almost all the space, so that the relatively small entrances make the smaller number of people who process on stage look as though they are a much larger crowd. He has also set the priests on one side and the women on the other so that their opposing choruses have a 'stereo' effect. (There are eight separate sets of words and music to be sung at the same time.)

The singers aren't in costume but they use real 'props' such as the trophies and victory crown. The King, princess and High Priest wear parts of their costumes, however, because they must learn to move in these unusually heavy outfits. Stage costumes may look like the real thing—in this case leather inlaid with gold—although they are only canvas and paint. They are often, as a result, heavier and hotter than the real thing.

The **set**—the scenery—is in position. The designer and master carpenter check that the ramps are not splintering wood, which might hurt the slave dancers' bare feet (**6**). Out in the stalls, the lighting designer tests the effects of different lights on the set. His work can only be completed when all the costumes are worn on the finished set: his lighting will change colours and throw shadows, and his work sometimes continues until the last minute before the performance.

Also on stage are the **stage managers** who will be responsible for directing the actual performance backstage (**7**). They mark a copy of the score with all the moments of entry or where the lighting or the scene changes. These are called **cues** and it's the stage managers' job to make sure that they happen in exactly the right place. They also control the curtain or **tabs** (it is electrically operated) so that it 'comes in' at the correct time. They work from the **prompt desk** (**8**), an electric panel which includes a television screen showing the conductor's desk and an intercom to make backstage announcements.

Beside them is the **chorus master**. During a performance, he can conduct choristers who can't see the conductor by watching on another television screen. (In the past, people relied on looking through holes in the scenery.) The conductor himself has been beating time for the singers, although only a pianist is in the pit (**9**); the full orchestra only attends for the final rehearsals. (He's worried that the singers will be unable to see him when they move as the producer has asked them to do. Often convincing dramatic movements have to be changed simply because the singers can't see the conductor: when the singers face the King, for example, they have their backs to him.)

Waiting for a word with the producer is someone from publicity with a draft of the First Night programme and from the management to say that an artist has telephoned to say he is too ill to rehearse. Waiting for the designer is someone from the wardrobe department to arrange a costume 'fitting' (when he can see a singer in costume).

The closer the final or **dress rehearsal** comes, more and more urgent decisions have to be taken. With three days to go, not only the performers are nervous.

Above, below and behind the stage

As we leave the rehearsal we look up to the dizzy galleries 70 feet above us where the cloth scenery, which is light enough to be hung on bars, is stored. During a performance, at a cue from the stage manager, the **cloths** can be **flown** in by the **fly-men,** by pulling on ropes and winches. The rest of the scenery is **built** on **trucks** of wood or metal and wheeled in from the sides and the back of the stage. A modern theatre might have twice as much storage space as the stage itself so that sets can be easily changed.

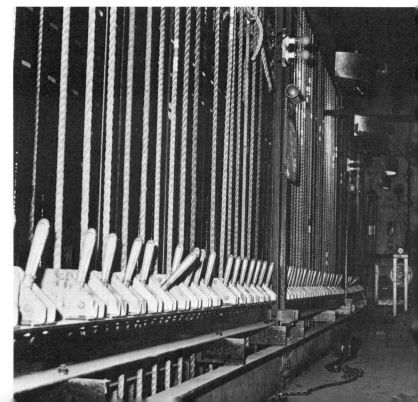

Immediately through the doors at the back of the stage are the dressing rooms—bleak, simple rooms with large mirrors surrounded by rows of naked light bulbs. There are primitive washing arrangements in most theatres, and showers are shared by many artists. Special care of hot water has to be taken during a show with a large cast!

Behind and above all this is a maze of staircases, corridors and offices. Below the stage is the staff canteen where stage hands and artists eat, drink and talk.

▼ Shifting scenery ready for the next production at the Vienna Opera House

Electrics and props

As soon as the morning rehearsal 'call' has finished on stage, the set for *Aida* will be **struck** (dismantled) and stored, possibly outside the theatre in a huge van. Then the set for the evening performance (a different opera entirely) will be built. The lighting for *Aida* has to be altered, so the lighting bars are dropped on the stage for the **LX (electrics)** crew to adjust. (When the set is ready, the lamps will be focussed by the crew on ladders.)

In the meantime, the **props** staff will lay out the props on each side of the stage. ('Props' are called properties because, in the past, they were often the personal property of actors.) Props

▼ Making a fibreglass statue. (1) Cutting the mould; (2) Coating the mould; *next page* (3) Gilding the statue; (4) The finished product

include anything the performers will carry on to the stage: swords, fans, books, glasses, letters, etc. In a complicated production, the props tables may hold several hundred items.

At about 5 pm, the cast will begin to arrive and the stage manager will check that everything is in order. Satisfied with everything, he will retire to dress in formal evening clothes for the performance: he is responsible for everything that happens backstage from half an hour before the curtain rises until after the performance, and must look smart because in an emergency he may have to make an announcement.

◄ The stage manager's props lists
▼

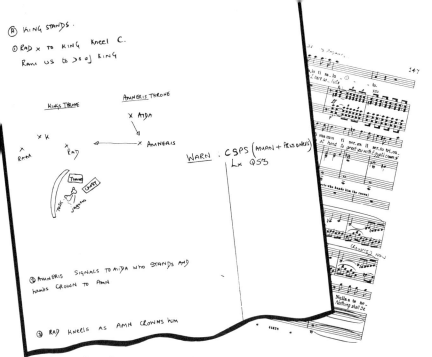

Ⓐ KING STANDS.
Ⓞ RAD x TO KING Kneel C.
Rami US to Ds of KING

KINGS THRONE

AMNERIS THRONE

X AIDA

X K

X AMNERIS

X RAD

X RAMI

WARN : CSPS (AMAN + PRISONERS)
Lx Q53

Ⓑ AMNERIS SIGNALS TO AIDA WHO STANDS AND hands CROWN TO AMN

Ⓒ RAD KNEELS AS AMN CROWNS him

▲ A page from the stage manager's prompt book and (below) the scene on stage

The performance

By the time the stage manager 'calls the half'—announcing that there is only half an hour before the 'beginners' call'—all the cast must be in the theatre. It is a theatre rule that the whole cast must be there when the show starts, even if they're only in the last scene. Singers need to warm up their voices by singing musical exercises, as well as to relax and get into costume and make-up. Many bring books, cards or knitting to pass the time while they're not on stage.

Stage management call the 'quarter' to warn everyone that there are 15 minutes to the 'beginners' call'; Wardrobe staff help

▼ The stage manager at his control desk

the singers put on their costumes and wigs: these 'dressers' suffer all the nerves of the artists' stage fright. It's their job to keep them happy—and jokes are essential.

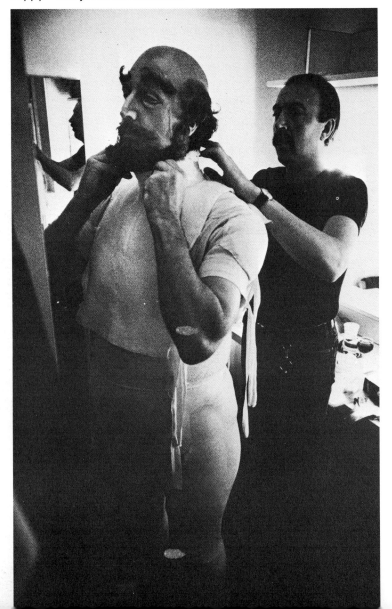

'Beginners please: Miss C, Ladies and Gentlemen of the Chorus, your five-minute call'. 'Ladies and Gentlemen of the Orchestra, your five-minute call'. The singers gather on stage and the musicians tune up in the pit. Then the conductor walks out alone into the pit, shakes the leader of the orchestra by the hand and bows to the applause of the audience. He turns back to the orchestra, and raises his baton for the performance to begin.

From the **wings** at the side of the stage, the stage manager calls the artists as they are needed. His score contains notes of all the **cues** he has to give. When he brings the curtain down at the end of the performance, he shouts out the order in which the artists take a bow to the audience, and decides on the number of 'curtain calls' by the amount of applause.

After the show, the artists leave the theatre quickly, unless they have visitors to entertain. Usually, the stage manager writes a short report on the performance (for the management to see next morning) and is the last to go. Only the fireman stays, unless the stage crew have to remove (**strike**) the set because at 8 am another set must be built, for a 10 am rehearsal. All-night shifts are tiring and very expensive so they rarely happen.

▼ The *Aida* costumes are so precious that they have to be hung on the wall out of harm's way

Questions

1a What and where is the pit? How many people can sit there?
 b Where is the lighting control box?
 c What and where is the prompt box?
 d What are the theatrical words for the curtain, the scenery, the area above the stage?
2 What is the dress rehearsal?
3 What do stage managers do?
4 Why are 'props' so called? What sort of things *are* props?
5 What does 'striking the set' mean?
6 What is the 'beginners' call'?

Projects

1 Draw a plan or make a model of the auditorium of an opera house showing stalls, balcony, gallery, amphitheatre, stage and pit. Label the tabs, the flies, the iron, etc.
2 Rehearse a short scene from a musical or play. First read it through, sitting down. Then ask yourselves why the characters act in this way and what short of atmosphere you want. What sort of design is necessary? Then work out some basic moves. If you don't have texts, improvise a scene on a subject you know about. Choose a scene with lots of action—a murder, an aeroplane crash, or the unexpected discovery of some money. Include some atmospheric music to create the mood of the scene, and compose a song to be sung by one or all of the characters at the climax.
3 Imagine you are just about to act as stage manager for an opera. Write a letter to a friend, or describe what you will need to do, in a taped interview, as if you were being interviewed for the radio.
4 Take a simple scene—from a film or TV story for example. Work out and list all the scenery, props and lighting effects you'd need for a performance. Then imagine that, because of expense, you can only use half of them. Which can go, and which must stay, if the performance is still to be a success?

▼ Striking the set after a performance

3 The people in opera

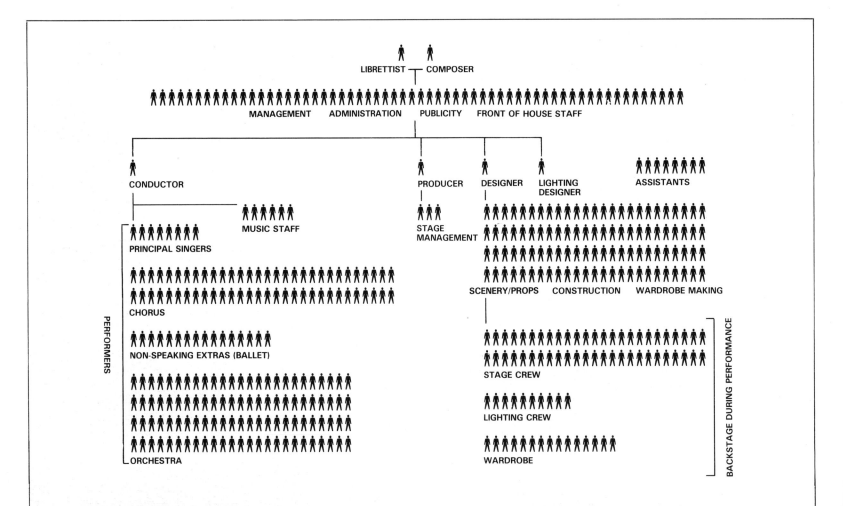

Opera has always been extravagant with manpower; one cause of its huge expense today is the large number of wages to be paid.

This chart shows all the different people who take part in the preparation of a new opera.

Librettist and composer

Let's take *Carmen* as an example of how an opera is written. The composer was Georges Bizet (1838-75), a brilliant musician with a talent for musical humour: he once set a whole newspaper (including the adverts) to music. He chose the subject of *Carmen* from a popular French novel and asked two well known playwrights to make a **libretto** (a text verion suitable for setting to music) out of it. Meilhac, who didn't care for music, wrote only the outline and the spoken words; Halévy wrote the verse for the opera's songs.

The French composer Georges Bizet ▼

Bizet encouraged the writers and the artists to bring out the shocking side of the drama. His own suggested words for Carmen's dance are stronger than Halévy's, and we may guess that he had already thought of the music before the words were written.

Bizet's librettists Halévy (left) and Meilhac (right) ▶

Not all librettos are adapted from novels. Sometimes composer and librettist will agree together on the details of an entirely new story, and create the opera from scratch. Some composers do away with librettists altogether, and write their own librettos (Wagner and the English composer Sir Michael Tippett are two examples)—but often a composer and librettist who work well together stay in partnership for several operas. Examples are Mozart and da Ponte, Verdi and Boito, and—less grand but even better known—Gilbert (words) and Sullivan (music). (See page 62.)

Composers and their librettists: (right) Sir Michael Tippett and ▶ (below) Mozart and Da Ponte ▼

Conductor

The conductor of an opera has two main jobs—(a) to train the singers and orchestra and (b) to conduct the actual performances. At the performance, he is the most important single performer because he beats time to keep everyone—orchestra, singers, chorus, dancers—together; even the stage manager follows his beat to signal all the stage effects. For this reason, he has the complete score of the opera in front of him, showing all the parts. He has to know where mistakes may happen: any one of the (perhaps) 250 performers may make a wrong entry and, somehow, he has to bring them together again. (At the first performance of *Carmen*, for example, the conductor had to cope with a bass drum entry two bars early in the middle of a soft passage!)

▼ The conductor (seated) working with the producer

The conductor has to judge and control the balance of sound from the pit and the stage. If the orchestra is too loud, the voices won't be heard, and both audience and singers will be furious. The conductor also controls the pace of the action and moulds the shape of the performance. If he allows too much excitement too early, he may lose a later climax; if he goes too slowly, he may lose the tension. As much as twenty minutes can be lost or gained over a four hour opera by different conductors!

All this responsibility can go to some conductors' heads. The composer Verdi once sourly protested, 'Conductors think they're so important that they almost believe they wrote the opera!'

Orchestra

Before 1800, an opera orchestra was small enough for one of the instrumentalists (often the composer at the harpsichord) to keep it together. In 1600 the orchestra numbered about 25 and in 1800 about 50; by 1900, operas had been written with whole symphony orchestras of over 100 players which had to be controlled by a conductor.

A place in an opera house orchestra is a secure job for an instrumentalist and takes up about 24 hours of the week (usually in the evenings). The players are expected to know the music when they arrive at the conductor's first rehearsal. Although an exceptionally difficult piece may call for extra orchestral sessions, the conductor can usually rely on players to be familiar with the best known works.

Some opera scores have very dull parts for the orchestra—the main interest is in the singing, and the orchestra plays plain accompaniments. But in the finest operas the power of the orchestra is fully used: to underline and increase the atmosphere, and to tell us things the character may be hiding (for example, the music he sings may be smiling and polite, but the orchestral

The pit at Bayreuth (the opera house founded by Richard Wagner for the ▶
performance of his music dramas)

accompaniment may show that he is boiling with fury underneath).

After one or two rehearsals for the orchestra alone, the singers will be called for a **sitzprobe** (sitting rehearsal). This is the first time they have sung the parts with the full orchestra, although they will have spent several weeks in rehearsals with piano accompaniment. So, with their scores open on their knees, they sing through their parts, to check any musical mistakes, and discover with how much orchestral sound they have to sing.

Producer

Unlike the conductor, the producer does not take part in the actual performance. His hard work has gone on beforehand, rehearsing the singers and arranging all the movements and dramatic action on the stage. At the performance, he need not even be there at all. His work is locked in the performers' memories; it is also written down in a 'production book' for future rehearsals so that, if necessary, the production can be polished or re-rehearsed by his assistants later on (for example if a new singer joins the cast).

Many opera producers are directors for film, television or the theatre. Their basic job is the same in opera—to sort out the production's dramatic movement—but opera has special problems. The most important difference is the music itself: the singers always need to see the conductor and to be in comfortable positions for singing. Sometimes the composer makes fantastic, impractical demands: it's easier for him to write instructions in his score like 'He disappears' or 'She flies away' than it is to carry them out effectively on stage.

Many singers with fine voices don't also possess natural acting talent. The producer has to train them to look relaxed on stage, to play their parts convincingly and to communicate what the composer wants. In the words of a great opera star, Maria Callas, 'If you're not sure what gesture to make on stage, listen to the music—the composer has thought of it for you'. It's the producer's job to help the singer put this advice into practice.

Designer, wardrobe and lights

The producer works closely with the designer to achieve the stage picture he or she wants. They use scale models (like toy theatres) of the sets to test their ideas. Alterations can be conveniently and cheaply made on the model, using matchsticks and old egg-boxes: the same changes would cost thousands of pounds on stage. While the designer is trying to satisfy the producer, he or she also has to bear in mind what will be practical to operate. Machinery must not squeak at vital moments. Quick scene-changes must not be difficult. The exits must be large enough for a chorus of 60 to empty the stage in seconds.

When designer and producer are agreed, the model is presented for approval and costing by the management. If making the set will be more expensive than the budget allows, or if the budget has been reduced, the designer's work starts again. The set should be under construction three or four months before the First Night.

▼ The set for Verdi's *Otello* and (inset) the designer's model

Designing opera costumes requires a similar eye for economy. Hundreds of costumes may be needed for one show, and some of them only for a brief scene. The clothes are made by experienced wardrobe staff—cutters—who interpret the designer's drawings. Experienced buyers shop in department stores or old clothes' markets for material, and visit the zoo if they need feathers and fur. They make armour out of fibre-glass and jewellery out of shoe and furnishing trimmings. Wardrobe work is full of surprises—most new materials, for instance, have to be 'broken down': that is, made to look old, as if the clothes have been worn for some time.

Designs for a production are not usually changed after the First Night—but a change of cast will involve new costumes to the

◀ A sketch for a costume
▼ (left) Spraying costumes to make them look old
(right) Making a head-dress

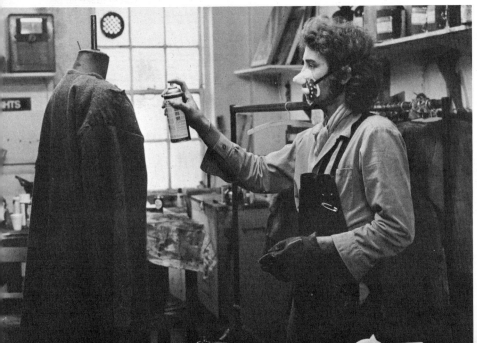

same designs. And a lot of maintenance and cleaning has to be done in the wardrobe between performances so that (for example) shirts are spotless and jackets are not creased. Everything is clearly marked and stored. Wigs (made of human hair) are also necessary. They are made and **dressed** by experts.

The right costume and wig reassure an artist and help his performance. Every care is taken to make sure they are comfortable enough to be worn under the hot stage lights and for singing—it is no good making a colourful or characterful costume that is too uncomfortable to wear.

Another designer plans the lighting of a production. He is an expert on the curious effects which the four or five hundred lights in the theatre can make. A gauze of fine net, for example, can be painted with a scene. When it is lit from in front, the audience sees only the picture; if it is lit both from in front and behind, artists behind the gauze will be seen as well; if it is not lit from the front but only behind, the gauze will be invisible and the artists perfectly clear. Special light bulbs can be made to flicker like flame; special moving lenses can be attached to create an underwater effect or a cloudy sky.

The bass Richard van Allan trying to relax in his costume for *The Italian Girl in* ▶
▼ Spraying a scenery gauze with paint
Algiers

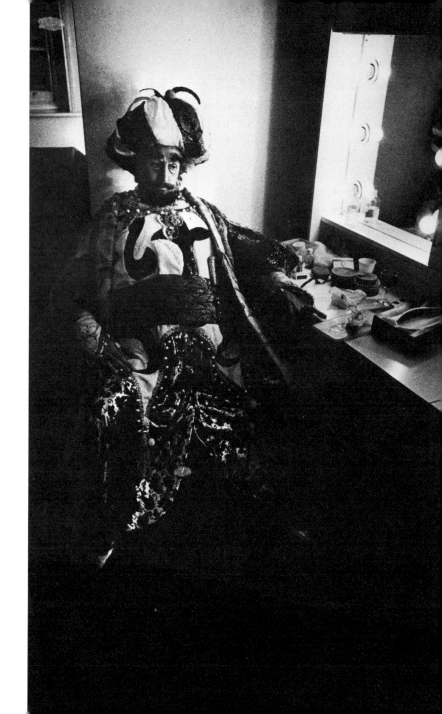

Questions

1 Which opera composers wrote the words of their operas?
2 Who is the librettist? Name a librettist who worked closely with (a) Mozart, and (b) Verdi.
3 What does a conductor do before and during the performance?
4 How big was an opera orchestra in 1600? In 1800? In 1900?
5 What is a *Sitzprobe*?
6 Describe the job of the producer.
7 What does the wardrobe department do?
8 Why is the designer's work so important?

▼ In the sound effects control box

Projects

1 How would you create the effect on stage of (a) a glass smashing into pieces, (b) someone being run through with a sword and bleeding, (c) someone disappearing?
2 Design a costume for the largest person you know to look very thin and for the shortest person you know to look very tall. Design a set for your school stage of a play or musical you know well. Find out how much it would cost in materials and how long it would take to build.

▲ Scene from the Drury Lane production of *The Pirates of Penzance* with Pamela Stephenson

3 With cat-like tread upon our prey we steal
In silence dread our cautious way we feel
No sound at all we never speak a word
A fly's footfall would be distinctly heard

Come friends who plough the sea
Truce to navigation take another station
Let's vary piracy with a little burglary

Here's your crowbar and your centre bit
Your life preserver you may want to hit
Your silent matches your dark lantern seize
Take your file and your skeletonic keys

(Repeat verses one and two.)
Read through these lyrics from the Gilbert and Sullivan opera *The Pirates of Penzance*. They have been slightly adapted in order to make them easier for you to set to music. Read them through a few times until the words suggest to you a definite rhythm. Each verse has a different rhythm or metre so try and compose a particular tune for each one and yet still make them sound as if they are a part of one song. Tape record your song, or, if you can, write it down in musical notation.

(Opposite) The Act 1 set design for the first performance of Bizet's *Carmen* in ▶ 1875

4 Six scenes from opera

The beginnings

The first operas were written for the courts of Northern Italy around 1600. They combined two earlier forms of entertainment: (1) spectacular 'interludes' in spoken plays which included choruses, solo singing and dance and (2) dance entertainments with music and song. The third (and new) element in opera was **recitative,** a kind of 'speech-song'. The aim was to recreate the effect of classical Greek theatre, and so the first operas were based on classical stories such as the story of Orpheus, the legendary musician who went down to hell to bring his wife back from the dead. Monteverdi's *Orfeo* is the first great opera (1607) and is still performed today.

Venice was the first city to open a public opera house and Monteverdi wrote his most important operas for this public. The fashion spread quickly over Europe, where the Italian operas of Monteverdi and others were much appreciated in aristocratic circles. But ordinary people wanted entertainments where they could understand what was going on, and so operas in the language of the audience were also in demand. Purcell's *Dido and Aeneas* was one of the earliest operas to be written in English.

◀ The Italian opera composer Claudio Monteverdi

▼ Set design for a spectacular entertainment called a masque (a forerunner of opera)

Henry Purcell (1659-1695)

Purcell was born into a musical London family and showed early signs of being very talented. As a choirboy in the Chapel Royal he learnt the traditional English vocal music and the newer Italian style for solo voices. He soon took to composition as well as playing the organ in the service of Charles II, James II, and William and Mary. He wrote hundreds of songs, anthems, and instrumental pieces. He composed for State occasions, such as Royal birthdays, weddings and funerals (for example, the *Ode to St Cecilia,* 1692, the *Elegy for Queen Mary,* 1694). Purcell was a popular figure in the theatre of the time. His theatrical entertainments such as *The Fairy Queen* (based on Shakespeare's *A Midsummer Night's Dream*) are called 'semi-operas' because they are really elaborate musical interludes to spoken plays. *Dido and Aeneas,* composed in 1689, was Purcell's only real opera.

Dido and Aeneas

Purcell wrote *Dido and Aeneas* not for the court for which he regularly composed, but for a girls' boarding school in Chelsea, run by a dancing master. He needed extra money and no doubt enjoyed this opportunity to experiment. He chose a subject which would have been popular with the girls—the love story of Dido and Aeneas from Virgil's Latin epic, the *Aeneid.* The pupils probably took part in the dances, the choruses and possibly even performed the main roles. Aeneas, the only male role, was not very important. The orchestra was probably professional.

The libretto was written by Nahum Tate, who added witches and jolly sailors' choruses to the tragedy, to make the opera more exciting for the audience—and the performers!

Purcell followed the French court opera style (established by the

▼ Costume design by Alexander McPherson for the chorus of witches in the English National Opera Production

composer Lully). These operas contained a lot of dancing and the drama progressed in **recitatives** (see page 30). But where Lully's chorus commented on the action without taking part in it, Purcell made his chorus central to the drama. He also added an Italian feature which had started with Monteverdi: a lament. Purcell began and ended his opera with this sort of song: Dido's famous lament 'When I am laid in earth', tells us a lot about her emotions and the result is very moving. The whole opera lasts less than an hour and it is difficult to stage because of the different scenes which follow one another quickly.

The story of Dido and Aeneas

Aeneas was a prince of Troy who escaped from the city when the Greeks destroyed it. The gods ordered him to sail to Italy and found Rome. His ship was swept ashore at Carthage, in North Africa, a great city ruled by the beautiful widowed Queen Dido. He fell in love with her and she, reluctantly, with him. In the opera a wicked sorceress who hates Dido conjures up a vision of the god Mercury to order Aeneas to abandon Dido and go to Italy.

In the final scenes, after the witches have enjoyed their triumph and the Trojan sailors have happily got ready to put to sea again, Aeneas comes to say goodbye to Dido. She hides her misery in anger. She tell him that his crocodile tears are as fake as his heart (**1**). When he begins to ask her to understand why he must go,

DIDO

Thus, on the fa-tal banks of Nile, Weeps the de-ceit-ful crocodile;

▼ Design for Aeneas's costume

▼ Sandra Browne as Dido and Christian du Plessis as Aeneas

DIDO
By all that's good, no more! All that's good you have for-swore.

AENEAS
By all that's good –

she scornfully interrupts, mimicking his musical phrase (**2**). She works herself into a passion and scornfully protests that she at least does not intend to change her mind, when he tells her that he will stay. She orders him to go. But once he has gone she tells her sister that she can only look forward now to death. The music is suddenly quiet and empty. A chorus (**3**) rounds off the scene with a philosophical comment on the lovers' quarrel. This prepares the mood of resignation to follow.

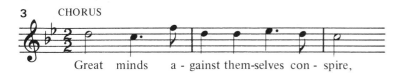

CHORUS
Great minds a-gainst them-selves con-spire,

DIDO
When I am laid, — am laid — in earth,

A feature of Dido's lament, 'When I am laid in earth' (**4**), is the slow rhythm of the **ground bass**. A ground bass is a short repeated musical phrase in the bass line with variations in the upper part. The solemnity of the lament contrasts with the quick angry scene before. Note how the repeated words and notes avoid monotony by subtle changes of rhythm and harmony. On the second refrain of 'Remember me, remember me' a bar's rest is lost, so that the accompaniment (heard first *between* the vocal phrases) clashes plaintively with the second 'remember me'. Purcell builds in his tragic effect by introducing sadly descending themes one by one. The important words ('laid', 'wrongs', 'trouble', 'remember' and the sighing 'ah') are stressed.

Questions

1a What are Purcell's other works for the theatre called? Why?
 b Which monarchs employed him?
 c Name one piece of music by Purcell apart from *Dido and Aeneas.*
2a What were the three elements of early Italian opera?
 b What effect were composers trying to recreate?
 c Name the first great opera, and say who wrote it. What is it about?

▼ Painting of Carthage by the English artist William Turner

3 Where was the first public opera house?
4a Why did Purcell write *Dido and Aeneas*?
 b Who founded the French operatic style?
 c What feature of the score of *Dido and Aeneas* is particularly Italian?
5 Where did Aeneas come from? Why did he go to Carthage? Where was it? Who was its queen? Why did he leave?

Projects

1

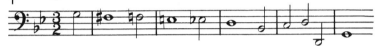

a This is the ground bass which occurs in the aria 'When I am laid in earth'. Listen carefully to a recording of it and then learn to sing or play it yourself. Suggest one or two reasons why the repetition of the bass line is never too obvious to the listener. Now try listening just to the ground bass and work out how many times the bass line is repeated.

b Listen to some of the other arias in this opera and try to find another one which uses a ground bass.

c Make up your own ground bass. Then work out some melodic variations which are musically suited to it.

2 Imagine you are Dido's sister. Write a diary account of Dido's love affair with Aeneas and the tragic end. Why do you think she was reluctant to fall in love with Aeneas? How did she kill herself? (The original story is in the *Aeneid,* Book IV.)

3 Design costumes for Dido and Aeneas. Remember that they are both royal—he is a hero, she is an empress—and that as they are drawn from a legend they do not have to belong to any particular historical period. How do you imagine the opera might have been presented at its first performance?

4 Find some other musical laments and listen to Monteverdi's *Arianna* if you can. Can you think of any pop songs about losing the person you love? Could you write one?

Wolfgang Amadeus Mozart (1756-1791)

Mozart was a child prodigy: from the age of four it was clear that he had outstanding musical gifts, and he toured Europe playing the harpsichord and composing for rich audiences everywhere. As a young man he worked briefly as court musician for the Archbishop of Salzburg, Austria, but he was literally kicked out and turned freelance. He settled in Vienna, and made his living from writing and performing music, and giving lessons. He wrote symphonies, concertos, sonatas, songs, church music and a dozen operas, including *The Marriage of Figaro* (1786), *Don Giovanni* (1787), *Così fan tutte* (Women are all alike) (1790) and *The Magic Flute* (1791).

The Marriage of Figaro

Opera before Mozart

During the 17th and 18th centuries in Europe, opera was mainly an entertainment for the rich. Rulers and princes competed with each other to pay for the most spectacular shows possible. Fine singers were as idolized and as well paid as pop stars are today. In this period there were strict rules governing the writing of operas. Stories had to be chosen from ancient history or classical mythology. Singers demanded music that would display their voices and stories that gave equal opportunities to each character: all the main parts had to have the same number of songs (**arias**) of equal length. So for a hundred years, libretti that conformed to all these rules were set to music over and over again by different composers.

▼ Cover of a piano score of Mozart's *The Marriage of Figaro* showing a scene with Cherubino the page boy

Mozart and opera

Some of Mozart's operas are written in this style. He began composing opera at the age of eight and naturally started by copying the most successful operas of his day. As he grew up, however, he wanted to produce works that were exciting not only musically, but dramatically as well. He realized that in opera the musician (not the librettist) must have the last word in how the action develops. And, of course, he added:

> The best thing of all is when a good composer, who understands the stage and is talented enough to make sound suggestions, meets an able poet; in that case no fears need be entertained as to the applause even of the ignorant.

Mozart's chance to write the kind of opera he wanted came when he met the Italian poet and librettist Lorenzo da Ponte. Da Ponte was a colourful character, a great storyteller, fond of the ladies and—some said—a boaster and a cheat. (He ended his life in New York, running a music academy.) Mozart and da Ponte

▼ The theatre in St Michael's Square, Vienna, where *The Marriage of Figaro* was first performed

decided to work together making an opera from *The Marriage of Figaro*. This was a French comedy of the time, very much in the news because Louis XVI banned it for immorality—a Countess is shown on stage accepting a page boy's proposals of love. Many of the characters also made thinly disguised speeches criticizing the current laws. For the same reason, Louis's brother-in-law the Austrian Emperor was reluctant to allow the play to be staged in Imperial theatres. Da Ponte declared it was bound to attract huge audiences because of its scandalous reputation—and he joked that what people were forbidden to say on stage, they could certainly sing.

The story of The Marriage of Figaro

The Marriage of Figaro centres on a Count who wants to exercise his right to make love to every girl on his estate before she

▼ (left) The first Susanna at Covent Garden in 1819 and (right) Poster for the first performance at Covent Garden

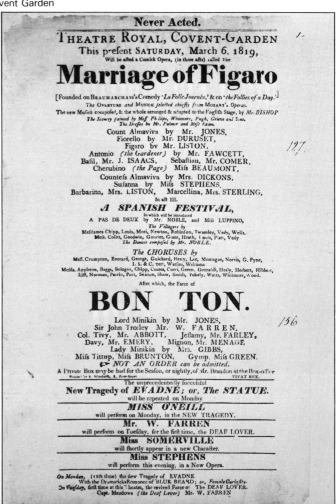

Never Acted.

THEATRE ROYAL, COVENT-GARDEN

This present SATURDAY, March 6, 1819,

Will be acted a Comick Opera, (in three acts) called the

Marriage of Figaro

[Founded on BEAUMARCHAIS's Comedy 'La Folle Journée,' & on 'the Follies of a Day.']

The OVERTURE and MUSICK selected chiefly from MOZART's Operas.

The new Musick composed, & the whole arranged & adapted to the English Stage, by Mr. BISHOP

The Scenery painted by Meff Philips, Whitmore, Pugh, Grieve and Sons.

The Dreffes by Mr. Palmer and Miss Egan.

Count Almaviva by Mr. JONES,

Fiorello by Mr. DURUSET,

Figaro by Mr. LISTON,

Antonio *(the Gardener)* by Mr. FAWCETT,

Bafil, Mr. J. ISAACS, Sebaftian, Mr. COMER,

Cherubino *(the Page)* Miss BEAUMONT,

Countess Almaviva by Mrs. DICKONS,

Susanna by Miss STEPHENS,

Barbarina, Mrs. LISTON, Marcellina, Mrs. STERLING,

In act III.

A SPANISH FESTIVAL,

In which will be introduced

A PAS DE DEUX by Mr. NOBLE, and Miss LUPPINO,

The Villagers by

Mesdames Chipp, Louis, Mori, Newton, Robinson, Twamley, Vedy, Wells,

Meff. Collet, Goodwin, Gouriet, Grant, Heath, Louis, Platt, Vedy

The Dances composed by Mr. NOBLE.

The CHORUSES by

Meff. Crumpton, Everard, George, Guichard, Healy, Lee, Montague, Norris, G. Pyne,

I. S. & C. Tett, Watson, Williams

Mesda. Appleton, Baggs, Bologna, Chipp, Coates, Corri, Green, Grimaldi, Healy, Herbert, Hibbert,

Liff, Norman, Parrio, Port, Sexton, Shaw, Smith, Tokely, Watts, Whitmore, Wood.

After which, the Farce of

BON TON.

Lord Minikin by Mr. JONES,

Sir John Trotley Mr. W. FARREN,

Col. Tivy, Mr. ABBOTT, Jeflamy, Mr. FARLEY,

Davy, Mr. EMERY, Mignon, Mr. MENAGE

Lady Minikin by Mrs. GIBBS,

Miss Tittup, Miss BRUNTON, Gymp, Miss GREEN.

☞ *NOT AN ORDER can be admitted.*

A Private Box may be had for the Seafon, or nightly, of Mr. Brandon at the Box-office

Printed by E. Macleish, 2, Bow-ftreet VIVAT REX.

The unprecedentedly successful

New Tragedy of EVADNE; or, The STATUE.

will be repeated on Monday

MISS O'NEILL

will perform on Monday, in the NEW TRAGEDY.

Mr. W. FARREN

will perform on Tuefday, for the first time, the DEAF LOVER.

Miss SOMERVILLE

will shortly appear in a new Character.

Miss STEPHENS

will perform this evening, in a New Opera.

On Monday, (11th time) the new Tragedy of EVADNE

With the Dramatick Romance of BLUE BEARD; or, Female Curiofity.

On Tuefday, first time at this Theatre, the revived Farce of The DEAF LOVER.

Capt. Meadows *(the Deaf Lover)* Mr. W. FARREN

marries. (This was still the law in France.) In particular, he wants Susanna, the pretty girl who is about to marry his manservant Figaro. The story of the opera tells how Figaro and Susanna plot to outwit the Count. It's a comic libretto with plenty of disguises, hiding in cupboards and mistaken identities. The political speeches in the play were not included in the opera. Instead, Mozart's music gives an extraordinary depth to each character, pointing out the sadness, bitterness and jealousy beneath the high-spirited comedy.

At its first hearing in Vienna, *The Marriage of Figaro* wasn't a great success. It was only when it was performed in Prague that it became popular. As Mozart wrote from that city:

I looked on with the greatest pleasure while people flew about in sheer delight to the music of my *Figaro,* arranged for quadrilles and waltzes. For here they talk about nothing but *Figaro.* No opera is drawing like *Figaro.* Nothing, nothing but *Figaro.* Certainly a great honour for me!

▼ The famous scene from Act III: (left to right) Bartolo, Marcellina, Figaro, Susanna, the Count, the Lawyer (Royal Opera House production)

A scene from Act Three

When the scene begins, there are five people on stage. Figaro, who owes money to an unattractive woman called Marcellina, has just been told by the lawyer that if he doesn't pay up he'll have to marry her. The Count, who has encouraged this plan to get rid of Figaro, can't wait till he's gone so that he can start flirting with Susanna, Figaro's bride-to-be. Marcellina's employer, an old man called Bartolo, has come along to see the fun.

All at once Marcellina gives a gasp of surprise. She has just recognized Figaro as her long-lost son—and not only that, but she announces that Bartolo is his father. Mozart now begins a long piece for all six singers, a sextet. Its form is like a musical arch: there is a first section, a contrasting second section and then the first section returns (in an altered and extended form). The piece is chiefly built on three musical ideas:

The flow of the music works like this: Marcellina begins (singing idea no. **1**), and Bartolo joins in (also singing **1**). The Count and his lawyer, meanwhile mutter their annoyance (singing idea **2**) that the plan to marry Figaro to Marcellina has unexpectedly gone wrong. Marcellina and Bartolo end this section by singing several time the words 'I'm your mother! I'm your father!' (**3**).

▲ Costume designs for *The Marriage of Figaro* (by Rosemary Vercoe)

Susanna now hurries in with money to pay Figaro's debt: this begins the second section of the sextet. She can't understand why Figaro and his new parents are happily singing (**3**), and jumps to the wrong conclusion when she sees Marcellina kissing Figaro. This musical section ends when Figaro tries to explain and Susanna shocks everyone by slapping his face.

The third section begins with Marcellina unravelling the mystery

1   Andante

MARCELLINA

Oh, my   long-lost child, em-brace me,
Ri - co - no - sci in que-sto am-ples-so

2

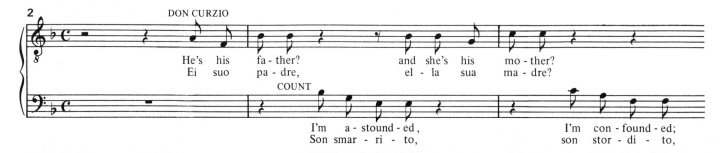

DON CURZIO

He's   his   fa-ther?   and she's   his   mo-ther?
Ei   suo   pa-dre,   el - la   sua   ma-dre?

COUNT

I'm   a-stound-ed,   I'm   con-found-ed;
Son smar - ri-to,   son stor - di-to,

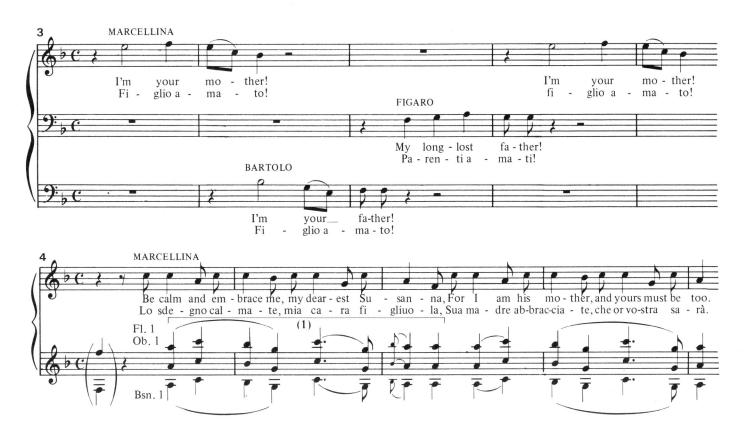

—(1) in the orchestra in example 4. Susanna sings of her amazement (2), and explanation and reaction are repeated several times to keep the comedy on the boil—the way Susanna turns the music of each answer upside-down, because she can't believe her ears before the characters confirm it and put the music the right way round, is particularly funny. At the end, Susanna has one more rising, questioning set of notes, as if she still can't believe her ears. But the sextet ends happily (5—compare the character of this music to 3) with everyone understanding one another.

The Act Three sextet shows how Mozart's music and da Ponte's words match perfectly. It was Mozart's own favourite scene from the whole opera.

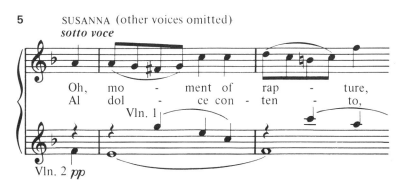

Questions

1 In what way did Mozart leave the service of the Archbishop of Salzburg? At what age did Mozart die?

2 What were the musical and dramatic ideas behind operas before Mozart's time? What sort of operas did Mozart want to write?

3 What made the original French play of *The Marriage of Figaro* controversial? What reason did the authorities in Vienna give for banning it? How did da Ponte think he and Mozart could get round this ban?

4 Figaro is the Count's manservant. What is his relationship with (a) Marcellina, (b) Susanna, (c) Bartolo?

Projects

1 Listen to a recording of the Act Three sextet from the opera. See if you can sort out the arch-construction of the music, using the musical ideas described in this section. Then explore the rest of the opera, on record or (if possible) at an opera house performance.

2 Find an English translation of the play *The Marriage of Figaro* (it's by Beaumarchais, and there's a Penguin Classics translation). With a group of friends, choose a scene, rehearse it and give a dramatic reading. It could be a scene later used by Mozart and da Ponte. Compare both versions. (You needn't sing the opera: just read the words of the libretto like a play. But put on a record of the music afterwards.)

3 Imagine you're the Count's lawyer, brought in to organize Figaro's wedding to Marcellina. Give a radio interview, or write a report to your employer, describing the extraordinary scene that took place after you broke the news of the wedding to Figaro. (Remember that the lawyer is a disapproving man with a stutter, who will not find comic high jinks at all amusing.)

4 Design scenery and costumes for Act Three of the opera. (It takes place in the Count's elegant house.) They can be 18th-century style (copied from books) or modern. What would a modern count wear? A lawyer? A doddery old man (Bartolo) — perhaps in a wheelchair.

5 The aria 'Non più andrai' ('Say goodbye now') occurs in Act One. The Count tells the page boy Cherubino, whom he has discovered in Susanna's room, that, as a punishment for eavesdropping, he is to join the Count's regiment. For a fun-loving page boy this is a terrible punishment, as Figaro points out to him when he sings the aria opposite.

The tune can be played on a recorder, piano or xylophone; guitar, piano, or xylophone can play the accompaniment. The bass line below can be played on a cello, guitar, bass xylophone or piano.

FIGARO

41

Georges Bizet 1838-1875

Bizet entered the Paris Conservatoire at the age of 10 and began composing two years later. In 1857 he won the Prix de Rome, a scholarship which enabled young artists to spend three years in Rome. He was not immediately successful as a composer and he spent much of his 20s making arrangements of other men's work. He composed *The Pearl Fishers* (1863) and *The Fair Maid of Perth* (1869), however, and won official recognition as a Chevalier de la Légion d'Honneur just before the disastrous première of *Carmen* and his death aged 37. If Verdi or Wagner had died at that age, we would scarcely remember them; Bizet, had he lived, might have been the greatest opera composer of his day.

Carmen

Carmen was written for a theatre in Paris called the **Opéra-comique.** This was not the main opera house, where the tradition of grand opera had developed. In grand opera no spoken dialogue was allowed; at the *Opéra-comique,* however, the songs and musical numbers were linked by spoken words. (Be careful! The name does not mean that the works performed there were comedies.)

Using spoken dialogue gives a composer the chance to introduce many different moods, and to tell his story faster between musical numbers. It raises the problem of when to break into music and song. Some incidents in *Carmen* are actually musical—the first act includes a march and two gipsy songs. Bizet introduces music at other moments, for example while the characters are still speaking, to set the scene, to whip up excitement, or to suggest emotions which cannot be expressed so deeply in words. The performers have to be excellent actors

▼ The *Opéra-comique,* where Carmen was first performed, was burned down in 1887; this engraving shows the panic-striken audience fleeing in all directions

because their speaking voices, as opposed to their singing voices, may not have been trained.

Although *Carmen* is one of the most popular of all operas today, it was not a success during the composer's lifetime. The chorus at the first production did not like the subject and complained about the difficulty of the music. The first night was a fiasco, partly because the audience objected to the 'shocking' immorality of the story and partly because the tenor who played Don José sang so badly out of tune that a harmonium had to accompany him. The disappointment affected Bizet's health. On the night of the 33rd performance, the singer playing Carmen became very distressed in the scene when Carmen reads her death in the cards. 'It is not for me that I am afraid', she said. Hours later Bizet was dead.

The story of Carmen

Bizet intended his opera *Carmen* to be 'something gay, which I shall treat as lightly as possible'. But he was in trouble from the beginning because not only was the subject thought to be very scandalous for the stage, but the heroine was not a virtuous soprano but a gipsy mezzo-soprano. As you have already read (page 21), Bizet constantly altered his librettists' attempts to smooth over the story.

Carmen tells the story of the love of a Spanish soldier, José, for a gipsy, Carmen. In his passion he forgets the girl his mother wants him to marry. He allows himself to be sent to prison for her sake, and to abandon his career, only to find that she tires of him and deserts him for the glamorous bull-fighter (Toreador) Escamillo. In despair he kills her.

A scene from Act One

The first act is set outside the barracks in Seville. The soldiers off duty and other townsmen gather to watch the girls who work in the tobacco factory. Above all they want to see the gipsy Carmen.

Carmen mocks the soldiers outside the barracks in Seville ▶

When she arrives (**1**), she flirts with them,

then launches into a slow gipsy dance called the *Habanera* to arouse their excitement.

Her first mocking words set the tone of her character. She, like love, is a wild bird that cannot be tamed. Bizet sets her speech in an easy rhythm which perfectly catches her self-confidence. The dance rhythm is Spanish (**2**): it is staccato, while the vocal line (**3**) smoothly descends across the beat. The music is menacing

because it is restrained; when it reaches a *forte* climax it quickly returns to *piano*; when the bass rhythm is broken the pause is tense with excitement (**4**).

At the end all the men surround her except for José. The quiet *tremolando* of the strings sounds with the theme known as 'Carmen's fate' (**5**). (It is heard also when she reads her death in the cards and when José kills her.) It is repeated higher and higher, as she approaches him. Carmen speaks over the music and, at the climax, throws a flower at José. She runs off laughing,

5 CARMEN'S FATE

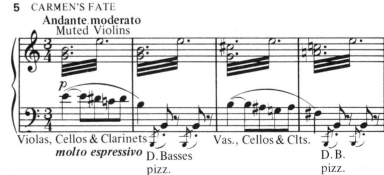

and the crowd repeat the words of her song for José's benefit: 'If I love you, take care!' With shouts of laughter and a loud orchestral tune, they disperse leaving him alone with the flower and the memory of her insolent challenge.

Questions

1 What is grand opera?
2 Why is Bizet's *Carmen* an *opéra comique* even though it has a tragic story?
3 Give two reasons why the first performance of the opera was a failure.
4 What kind of voice is the part of Carmen written for? Why was this unusual in opera in 1875?
5 Name the two male principals in *Carmen*. Which of them sings the famous Toreador's Song?

Projects

1 Design a poster to advertise *Carmen*. Remember all the different characters (gipsy girls, bullfighters, soldiers) and the story about love, jealousy and murder.
2 The Toreador's Song (page 46).
   This song is sung by Escamillo, the famous bullfighter, in Act Two. When he appears the crowd cheer him. He replies with this song which tells of the excitement of bull-fighting.
      You can play the tune on the recorder and piano. The bass line can be played on the piano, guitar or cello. Guitars can play the chords written above the tune.

Cover of a piano score of *Carmen* showing the square in Seville ▶

Allegro moderato

(Simplified version)

3 The Habanera

Opposite is an arrangement of the *Habanera* sung by Carmen in Act One when she first appears on stage. This aria introduces Carmen's wild and flirtatious character. As she sings Carmen tries to attract the attention of Don José.

The tune can be played on the recorder or piano. The accompaniment part can be played on the xylophone or chime bars. The piano, guitar, cello, and bass xylophone would be suitable for the bass line below.

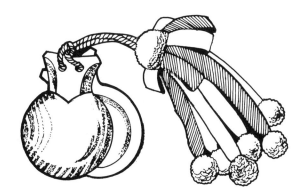

	Play this section once only.			This section is to be played four times before ending on								C
Count	① 2	① 2	① 2	① 2	① 2	① 2	① 2	① 2	① 2	① 2	① 2	① 2
Bass Line	C	C	C	C	C	C	C	C	C	C	G	C

Giuseppe Verdi (1813-1901)

Verdi, son of an innkeeper, was trained as a choirboy and church organist. He tried at first to get work as a cathedral musician in Milan, Italy, but his first opera was performed when he was 26, and after that he earned his living writing for the stage. He wrote 27 operas altogether, the last of them (*Falstaff*) when he was 80 years old. At least 15 of them are still regularly performed all over the world, and include some of the most popular and well-known operas ever composed: *Rigoletto* (1851), *Il trovatore* (1853), *La Traviata* (1853), *Don Carlos* (1867), *Aida* (1870) and *Otello* (1887). Apart from operas, Verdi's main composition is the huge Requiem Mass for soloists, chorus and orchestra.

Il trovatore

Verdi's operatic ideas

Verdi took his plots from many sources in history and literature, but never from legends of gods and heroes: whatever the context—the Crusades, Ancient Egypt, Shakespearean England, 19th-century Paris—he aimed to create human characters, reacting in a way which everyone could understand. Anger, fear, joy, love and revenge were to Verdi the same for all people, whether they were princes or peasants.

He also prided himself on his tunes. Italian singers came to expect show pieces for their voices in an opera, an opportunity to soar above the orchestra. Verdi, of course, had no time for singers who put their own importance before his operas! But he had a genius for writing for voices; and in particular for combining emotional strength and superb tunes. He was prepared to sacrifice a beautiful effect for one that was dramatically powerful, and this is why he is such a great composer for the theatre.

▼ Cartoon of Verdi rehearsing a scene from one of his operas, *A masked ball*

Verdi chose an extravagant, passionate Spanish play of love and revenge as the subject of his ninth opera. He described it as 'something original and out of the ordinary'. In fact, the story of *Il trovatore* (which means 'The troubadour') is one of the most unlikely in all opera—so much so that the Marx Brothers chose it to make fun of it in their film *A Night at the Opera.*

What attracted Verdi, however, was its colour and excitement. *Il trovatore* was a huge success at the time, and has remained so ever since. The music sweeps the audience along at such a pace that there is no time to worry about the unlikeliness of the plot.

The story of Il trovatore

Azucena, an old gipsy woman, has sworn revenge on the family of the Count di Luna (a powerful general of the Spanish King) because they burned her mother as a witch. She stole the Count's

▼ A design for the gipsy costume by Stefanos Lazaridis

◀ The old gipsy Azucena
(played by Fiorenza Cossotto)

baby brother but, in a terrible fit, confused him with her own child—and threw her own son into the fire. She brought up the other baby as her own son, Manrico; and he is now the Count's rival in love for the noble and beautiful Leonora. She loves him and, in the course of the opera, agrees to marry him.

As they prepare for the service, however, news arrives that the Count has captured Azucena. Manrico rushes off to rescue her. He fails and is thrown into prison with her. Leonora realizes that she can only save his life by persuading the Count that she will marry him. She then takes poison. The Count sees that she has tricked him and executes Manrico. Azucena collapses, screaming that he has killed his own brother: 'Mother, you are avenged!' The Count, cause of the deaths of his brother and the woman they both loved, is left alone and horror-struck as the curtain falls.

A scene from Act Four

Act Four begins with Leonora (soprano) outside the tower where her lover Manrico (tenor) is imprisoned, awaiting execution. She has come secretly at night to try to save him, but she has a ring with poison hidden in it to drink if she fails. She sends away her guide and thinks of Manrico as she sings a sad, slow aria (1). The orchestra supports the voice with gentle rhythms and delicate harmonies—notice how the violins accent the rising notes of the melody and leave the voice unaccompanied as it falls away.

A bell begins to toll and monks chant a lament (*Miserere*) (2) for those about to die. The rhythm (♩ 𝅘𝅥𝅯 𝅘𝅥𝅮 𝅘𝅥𝅯 𝅘𝅥𝅮) of almost the full orchestra and bass drum suggests a march to the scaffold. The menacing effect is increased by the fact that we can imagine but cannot see the monks' chorus.

Leonora's floating melody abruptly changes as she sings of her anxiety for Manrico. In a short repeated theme (3) she grows more and more frightened. The drum-beat increases the tension. Finally

◀ The famous soprano Adelina Patti as Leonora in *Il trovatore* she breaks down in 'sobbing' triplets (♪𝅘𝅥𝅮𝅘𝅥𝅮 ♪ 𝅘𝅥𝅮𝅘𝅥𝅮). At that critical moment, Verdi introduces the tenor voice of the troubadour Manrico, singing one of his most famous tunes (**4**). It is a heroic melody, just right for a man who is a passionate lover even in the face of death. Leonora hears him, although he (in his prison) cannot hear her.

Her reply is fast and agitated (**5**), excited that he is so close and yet so far away. The three tunes combine to create a huge climax centred on the lonely figure of Leonora onstage, torn by the sounds (offstage) of the death knell and Manrico's love song.

1
LEONORA

2
THE *MISERERE*

3
LEONORA

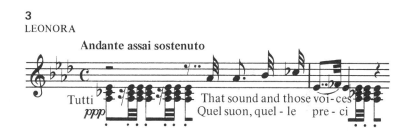

4
MANRICO

5
LEONORA

Censorship

Excitement in the theatre often worried the authorities responsible for good order in the State. Verdi had regular rows with the censors who wanted to cut out passages likely to upset the audience. The Catholic Church also objected to any mention of religious matters (for example burning at the stake), or even a passing reference to the devil. However idiotic the censors' objections may appear to us (or to Verdi) they could often be avoided by changing the names and setting in a libretto, without damaging the drama at all! In this way a 16th-century French king became a Duke of Mantua (in *Rigoletto*), or Gustav III of Sweden became the 17th-century British governor of Boston (in *A masked ball*)!

Questions

1 What ideas did Verdi think important in the writing of opera?
2 What special quality attracted Verdi to *Il trovatore*?
3 Name Verdi's last opera.
4 What other operas did Verdi compose within two years of *Il trovatore*?
5 What have his operas *Macbeth*, *Otello* and *Falstaff* got in common?
6 Censors often objected to Verdi's operas. Why?

Projects

1 Listen to a recording of the last act of *Il trovatore*. Follow it in a libretto or a score if you can. Then answer the following questions:
   a What type of voice is performing (a) Leonora's aria (**1**), (b) Manrico's aria (**4**)?
   b What sort of accompaniment does Verdi use to back up the soloists?
   c Which orchestral instruments do you notice?
   d At what points in the story is the music loud? And quiet?
   e What kind of atmosphere is the music creating?
   Afterwards, explore the rest of the opera, on record or in an opera house performance.
2 Write a letter to the censor who disapproved of *Il trovatore*.

Explain why you agree or disagree with the points he makes. Are there other things to be said as well?
3 Draw or model the scene: at night, a prison tower in enemy territory, a beautiful inexperienced girl desperately looking for her lover.
4 The papers are filled every day with stories of passion, love, murder, and revenge. Would any of them make the basis for an opera or play? Working with a group of friends, see if you can develop a newspaper story into a dramatic entertainment.

▼Design for the tower where Manrico is imprisoned in the last act

The Valkyrie

Music drama

Although he wrote his first operas in traditional style, Wagner's greatest works are all in an operatic form he invented himself, and which he called **music drama.** He was interested in the drama of the ancient Greeks (in which it was thought that actors chanted plays based on ancient myths, with a commentary from a chorus). He set out to develop this effect, using German myths and a symphony orchestra instead of the Greek chorus. He wrote music dramas on the legends of Tristan and Isolde, Parsifal and *The Ring of the Nibelung,* a 19-hour marathon work consisting of four linked music dramas (*The Rhine Gold, The Valkyrie, Siegfried* and *Twilight of the Gods*).

Wagner's music dramas were hugely ambitious in scope. He insisted on supervising everything himself: he wrote the words and the music, produced the operas, dictated what the scenery, lighting and costumes should be, and conducted many of the performances. He thought that a true music drama should join together music and all the other arts (words, painting, performing) into a 'total art-work' which would engulf its audience with grandeur and magnificence.

Bayreuth

No traditional theatre was suitable for Wagner's 'total art-works'. (The orchestra for *The Ring of the Nibelung* is vast, over 120 players, and takes up a huge amount of space: there are, among other things, no less than six harps.) So he decided to build a theatre of his own, to be used only for his music dramas.

He chose a small German town called Bayreuth as the site for his theatre—and for the Wagner festivals he meant to hold there every year. Then he began to raise funds to build the theatre by conducting special 'Wagner concerts' all over Europe. The money gradually came in, and at last the Bayreuth theatre—only a temporary wooden one, to an entirely original design by Wagner himself—was constructed and the first complete performance of *The Ring* was given in 1876. The audience of royalty, musicians and devoted Wagner fans applauded the venture as a triumphant success.

Although Wagner himself never saw *The Ring* performed at Bayreuth again, there is still an annual festival of his works given at Bayreuth every year. The theatre is now directed by his grandsons—and still operates in the temporary building constructed over a century ago.

Leading themes

Wagner devised the idea of 'leading themes' or **leitmotifs**. Each character and each idea in the drama has its own theme, sometimes a few notes, sometimes a whole tune. Whenever Wagner wanted to draw attention to the character or idea, he wove its theme into the musical texture.

Sometimes this is done very simply. Whenever the hero Siegfried appears, for example, we hear the Siegfried theme. But it

can also be extremely subtle. A character might be singing, for example, of loyalty and trust—and the orchestra, by playing the 'treachery' theme underneath, tells us to be on our guard. In this way, the orchestra (Wagner said) takes the part of the chorus in ancient Greek drama, pointing out the true meaning of the action. The audience is able to understand the precise meaning of the drama without need of words.

From the 'leading themes' Wagner built up a continuous web of music, unlike the musical structure which Mozart and Verdi (in different ways) had used. They chose dramatic situations which exactly matched recognizable musical patterns—so exactly that music. Mozart and Verdi chose dramatic situations which exactly matched recognizable musical patterns—so exactly that music and the drama develop naturally together. Wagner, on the other hand, made up entirely new musical forms to suit his dramas.

Stage effects in The Valkyrie

On the summit of a rocky mountain, clouds fly past as if driven by storm. In a flash of lightning, a Valkyrie on horseback becomes visible: on her saddle hangs a slain warrior . . .

▼ The theatre at Bayreuth in 1875 before the first performance of *The Ring*

▼ The Rhine maidens from the first Bayreuth performance of *The Rhine Gold* in 1876

These are Wagner's stage directions from the score of the second opera in *The Ring of the Nibelung, The Valkyrie.* The Valkyries were the beautiful warrior maids of German legend, daughters of the chief god, Wotan. Their job was to pick up the dead bodies of heroes from the battlefields and carry them on their

▼ (top) The Valkyrie in Act III of the 1913 Covent Garden performance and (below) in a modern performance

flying horses to the gods' victory hall in the heavens. The leader of the Valkyries was called Brünnhilde.

These stage-directions are ambitious—how do you show flying horses and warrior-maidens on an ordinary theatre-stage? In the 1876 Bayreuth performances, projected slides were used—and Wagner was by no means satisfied: 'Costumes, scenery, everything must be done anew for the repeat performance'. Modern productions often use the most advanced electrical equipment—for example, laser beams—to obtain the kind of effects Wagner imagined but could never have had in a 19th-century theatre.

The story of the opening of Act Three of The Valkyrie

The famous Ride of the Valkyries opens the last act of the opera. The two *leitmotifs* (1, 2) vividly describe the horses galloping through the air and landing on the mountain top where the Valkyries have chosen to meet. They laugh about their adventures: then a new theme (3) announces Brünnhilde's

4

DRAGON

Sehr schnell und heftig (very strong and fierce)

B. Clt.
Hns. &
Bsns. *p*

5

TREASURE (THE RING)

Sehr schnell und heftig

Clt., B. Clt.
& Hns. *p*

6

SIEGFRIED

Sehr lebhaft und schnell (very lively and fast)

Hns. *p*

7

SIEGLINDE (REDEMPTION THROUGH LOVE)

Sehr lebhaft und schnell

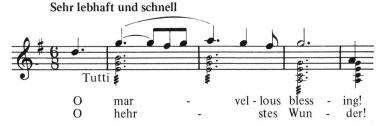

Tutti

O mar - vel - lous bless - ing!
O hehr - stes Wun - der!

approach. They are horrified when they hear that she has dared to disobey Wotan, by trying to save a hero from death. She brings the hero's wife with her and asks for a new horse so that they may escape. Wotan is chasing them. Sieglinde, the hero's wife, at first interrupts to say that she no longer wants to live (since her husband is dead). When Brünnhilde tells her that she will have a child, however, she begs to be saved. The Valkyries advise her to make her way on foot to the woods where a dragon (**4**) guards his treasure (**5**). Brünnhilde promises to stay behind and delay Wotan. She tells Sieglinde that her child will be the world's most glorious hero (**6**), gives her the pieces of his father's sword for him and tells her to call him 'Siegfried' (which in German means 'Victory-Peace'). Sieglinde thanks Brünnhilde (**7**) and escapes just as Wotan arrives in a thunder cloud. The Valkyries wail with fear at his approach.

This scene clearly shows how Wagner uses the *leitmotifs*. Each one (1-7) reappears in the cycle when its subject is mentioned. So, for example, Sieglinde's joyful theme (**7**) returns at the end of the last opera (*Twilight of the Gods*) to remind us that the world will be saved through love.

The scene also shows how opera can make legend work on stage. It is the music that makes us believe in flying horses and heroes and gods. They represent the forces which drive us ordinary people. The restless energy of the Valkyries and their horses, for instance, represents the wild side of Wotan's character—the side which he tries to control. We also feel its pull. Music has an advantage over words in appealing to our instincts directly.

Questions

1 What ideas from Greek drama did Wagner particularly admire?
2 What jobs did Wagner himself do in preparing for a performance?
3 Where is the Wagner Festival Theatre? What is it made of? Name one unusual feature of it? Who runs the Festival now?
4 What are leading themes? How are they used?
5 Who were the Valkyries? Who was their father? In what mythology did they appear?

Projects

1 Listen to a recording of Act Three of *The Valkyrie,* following it in a libretto or score. Keep an eye on the leading themes mentioned in this section, and see if you can identify them each time they occur. Move on to explore the rest of the opera, on record or in an opera house performance.
2 Make up leading themes to fit the different characters and ideas of a school day. (Head teacher? Maths? Boredom? Friendship? Getting out of school?) If you made the events of one day into a music drama, how often would each theme be used?
3 If you were staging *The Valkyrie* scene without slides or laser beams, with the ordinary things available to most school drama, how would you create the effects? Ask your drama teacher to suggest ideas. Write down a 'technical description' of how each effect would be created: thunder, lightning, storm-clouds, flying horses. (Then think about *The Rhinegold,* the first part of Wagner's *Ring*: *its* first act takes place underwater, with the characters swimming and diving like human fish. How can that be done on stage without drowning the singing—or the singers?)

Benjamin Britten (1913-1976)

Britten began writing music when he was seven; he later worked some of his childhood pieces into the *Simple Symphony.* He was highly successful as a composer, and earned his living from writing music (not an easy thing to do) from the time he was 18. He wrote particularly well for the voice, and composed many sets of songs and other vocal works. In 1948, he founded the Aldeburgh Festival in the seaside town where he lived. His works include 15 operas (among them *Peter Grimes,* 1945, and *A Midsummer Night's Dream,* 1961), concertos, a symphony, the *Serenade* (1943) for tenor, horn and strings, the *War Requiem* (1962), and many works for schools including the opera *Noye's Fludde* (1958).

Peter Grimes

Opera in Britain

From the earliest days of opera in the 17th century until today, opera has always been popular in Britain. Over the centuries, there have been periods when the best performances in Europe could be heard in London. Many British composers have composed operas. The most famous are Purcell (1659-95), Handel (1685-1759)—who spent all his career in London although born in Germany—and Sullivan (1842-1900)—who wrote popular comic operas with W.S. Gilbert, such as *The Mikado* and *The Gondoliers.*

To celebrate the reopening after the Second World War of Sadler's Wells Theatre in North London in 1945, a new work was performed. It was *Peter Grimes,* the second opera of Benjamin Britten. The first-night success established him immediately as a leading composer and he went on to write another 14 operas. He constantly tried to find new ways of matching words and music to make drama work for audiences today: he wrote an opera for television (*Owen Wingrave*), several children's operas and his last, *Death in Venice,* involves an unusual blend of dance and singing.

One of the most important inspirations of Britten's music was the atmosphere of his beloved native county, Suffolk. Because he was a pacifist (someone who doesn't agree with fighting wars) he went to live in America in 1939. But he was too homesick to stay abroad for long, and in 1942 he returned and went to live in Aldeburgh, Suffolk. While abroad he had read a poem, *The Borough,* by the 18th-century poet, George Crabbe, which is about a Suffolk fishing village. The character which caught Britten's imagination was a lonely, brutal fisherman at odds with his neighbours. Peter Grimes becomes, in the opera, a much more poetic character—a man with special insight beyond the narrow-minded, mean villagers of the fishing community.

The title role of *Peter Grimes* was written for the tenor, Peter Pears, Britten's life-long friend and companion. This illustrates a point true of older operas as well—that composers often find inspiration in their performers for the characters, and even for the subjects of their operas. Many famous operas (and other musical works too) have been written with the composers' friends in mind.

▼An old photograph of the fishing village of Aldeburgh

The story of Peter Grimes

Grimes is a fisherman in a small 19th-century fishing village. He is hated and feared by the villagers, because his grim, unsmiling ways have given him a reputation for cruelty. The opera begins with an inquest on one of his boy apprentices, drowned at sea. Grimes takes another apprentice, but the child is terrified of him, runs over a cliff in the darkness and is killed. The villagers think that Grimes is nothing but a monster: only Ellen, who cares for him, sees that he is shy and lonely. Finally, because of the boy's death, the villagers hound him until he sets out to sea in a storm, sinks his boat and drowns. Once the outsider is gone, the life of the village returns to normal.

A scene from Act One

The second scene of Act One opens with an orchestral piece painting the picture of a storm at sea. The action of the scene takes place in the village pub, where the villagers are sheltering after closing time. When the door opens, we hear the howling gale outside (1). The different village characters are picked out, rather

as a film cameraman might use a 'close up' on a crowd. There is Mrs Sedley who makes herself out to be too good for the company; there is Captain Balstrode who flirts with the Landlady's two 'nieces', and the girls themselves who say everything together and even giggle at the same time. Bob Bowles, the Methodist preacher, is drunk although he is supposed not to drink

▼ The villagers in the pub (Act 1 Scene 2) in the first production at the Sadler's Wells theatre in 1945

▼ Peter Grimes (played by Jon Vickers) and his boy apprentice in a recent production at Covent Garden

2

Adagio (♩ = 33)
sostenuto
PETER *pp*   *poco cresc.*

Now___ the Great Bear and Plei-a - des ___ where earth moves Are draw-ing up___ the clouds of hu-man grief ___

3

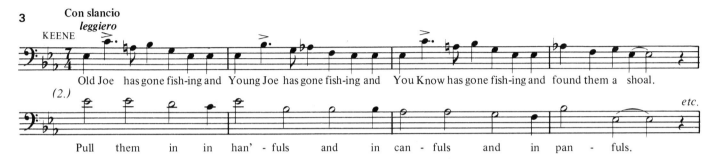

Con slancio
leggiero
KEENE

Old Joe has gone fish-ing and Young Joe has gone fish-ing and You Know has gone fish-ing and found them a shoal.

(2.)   *etc.*

Pull them in in han' - fuls and in can - fuls and in pan - fuls.

4   Presto con fuoco

Brass *fff*   Str. *ff*   *espr.*

alcohol. They're all waiting for a cart to arrive bringing goods from the town and a new apprentice for Peter Grimes.

Grimes himself appears. The villagers comment on his strange behaviour. He's absorbed in his loneliness, which he compares to the silence of the stars (**2**). The landlady (generally known as 'Auntie') fears that the bad feeling against Grimes may break out in a fight, since some of the men are drunk. She tells Ned Keene to start a song to distract attention from Grimes.

Ned begins an old English folk song, 'Old Joe has gone fishing', which everyone sings as a 'round' (**3**). When Grimes sings, he widens the musical intervals of the theme so that his part is clearly

separate from the rest.

Then the cart arrives with the new apprentice, and Ellen, the schoolmistress who went to fetch him. The storm still rages outside; a bridge has been washed away (**4**). Grimes horrifies everyone by his determination to set off with the boy immediately for his hut. 'Home!' cry the villagers together, scornfully: 'Do you call that home?' And on that, Grimes pushes the terrified boy out into the rain.

Britten dramatizes this scene by contrasting in his music the furious weather outside with the snug warmth inside. We feel the danger of the gale and the floods. He also pushes the action along very fast to obtain the 'feel' of pub conversation: we hear snatches from the general noise. He distinguishes Grimes's position from the others by giving him a different sort of music to sing: it is slow and passionate where theirs is rapid and chattering.

He introduces the 'round' so that the tune and the rhythm gradually take over the other music: the principle of a round is that each singer enters a certain number of beats after the one before and sings the same theme, around and around. It is great fun. A final point to notice is how he builds up the climax at the end: the hurried exclamations give way to a loud unison chorus of dismay.

Questions

1 Name a British opera composer of (a) the 17th century, (b) the 18th century, (c) the 19th century.
2 Where did Britten come from? Why did he go to America? Why did he return?
3 Where is *Peter Grimes* set? When was it first performed? Who sang the title role?
4 Name some of Britten's other compositions.
5 What do the villagers think of Grimes's behaviour and character, and the reasons for it? What does Ellen think?

Projects

1 Listen to a recording of *Peter Grimes,* Act One, following it in the libretto or score. Before you start, listen to or sing the round 'Old Joe's gone fishing' (music on page 60). As you hear the opera, see how Britten works the round into his musical texture. Then explore the rest of the opera, in a recording or an opera house performance.
2 Imagine you're a local newspaper reporter, writing an account for your paper of the terrible storm and the three recent deaths (two apprentices and Grimes). Your headline might be along the lines of SEA CLAIMS THREE LIVES—and you'd want to tell your readers something of the villagers' feelings about Grimes, and their suspicions about the apprentices' deaths. Would you also interview Ellen, to get a different point of view?
3 Draw a scene from the opera: the pub scene, or perhaps a stormy fishing scene at sea. (Use photos and pictures to make your figures, clothes and boats as 19th-century as you can.)
4 Make up a story of your own about an 'outsider' of the present day: you could set it in industry (the mines, a factory, the union), or make it a political story (refugees? spies?). Why is your hero an outsider, and what do other people think of him? How does the confrontation end? Can you find folk music (rounds and other songs) to build into your drama?

Conclusions

It should be clear by now that there are many ways of combining words and music, not all of them as serious as the ones described in this book. In the Middle Ages, dancing and singing were part of travelling minstrels' skills, and later on a tradition of comic and fantastic mimes and clowns flourished all over Europe. In the 16th-century Italian courts where operas began, dancing and spectacle were just as important as music.

In the last century, with the increasing number of people who could afford to go to the theatre, theatre managers saw growing demand for light entertainment. In England the successful

▼ A romantic moment from the film version of the Viennese operetta *The Merry Widow* by Franz Lehár

▲ Medieval entertainers

partnership of Gilbert and Sullivan, and their manager Sir Richard D'Oyly Carte, made light opera (or **operetta** as it is called) all the rage. Gilbert's comedies made fun of the stories of grand opera, while Sullivan's scores made fun of its music. In *The Gondoliers* two babies were confused at birth (compare Verdi's *Il trovatore* on page 49); in *Iolanthe* the Queen of the Fairies and her fairy subjects wore helmets and armour like Wagner's Valkyries.

In Vienna sentimental comedies such as Johann Strauss's *Die Fledermauns* (1874) were popular. This tradition eventually led to spectacular American musicals such as *Oklahoma!* or *My Fair Lady.*

Jazz has also made a contribution to opera. The negro spirituals and jazz rhythms of Gershwin's *Porgy and Bess* (1935) are the musical basis for an opera about negro slum dwellers. Sound amplification, electronic display and modern pop musicians bring spectacle, words and music together in **rock opera**. Even the life of Christ has been staged in *Jesus Christ Superstar,* with music by Andrew Lloyd Webber and words by Tim Rice. The life of a fascist dictator makes an equally successful show, *Evita,* by the same partnership.

Serious composers whose music does not need to have commercial appeal (because they work for state-financed companies) have been freer to experiment with more daring techniques than pop musicians. Subjects range from the conflict between East and West and racism (Tippett's *The Ice Break*), exorcism (Penderecki's *The Devils*), the visions of a medieval saint (Tavener's *Thérèse*) to communism, feminism, and black slavery.

Audiences do not flock to hear these operas as they do to a performance of Bizet's *Carmen.* But, like *Carmen,* which was not a success in the composer's lifetime, will they fill the theatres in 100 years' time? Or should an opera be judged on its immediate box-office appeal, such as that enjoyed by rock operas like *Evita?* This is what Verdi thought:

Read most attentively the reports of the box office. These, whether you like it or not, are the only documents which measure success or failure, and they admit of no argument and represent no mere opinion but facts . . . The theatre is intended to be full and not empty.

What do you think?

Questions

1 What do operettas, musicals, rock operas and operas have in common? What are the differences between them?
2 Who wrote *Porgy and Bess*? See if you can find out anything else he wrote.
3 Name two modern operas. If you can listen to some of their music and read about them, compare the ideas with rock operas.

◀ A poster for *The Mikado.* You can find an arrangement of one of its best known tunes on the next page

Projects

1 'Mi-ya-sa-ma' is sung in Act Two of *The Mikado* by Gilbert and Sullivan. The Mikado, the Ruler of Japan, has been told that his long-lost heir is hiding in Titipu. In order to find out the truth he comes to Titipu with his troops. The march 'Mi-ya-sa-

ma' announces the arrival of the Mikado and the inhabitants of Titipu bow down and express their loyalty through their singing.

Both the tune and accompaniment parts can be played with the following instruments: a xylophone, piano, recorder, guitar or chime bars.

2 Try to compose your own opera.

a. First decide on a plot. One way to do this is to look at plots of famous plays, legends, or people and incidents from history; stories from the Bible, about Count Dracula, or based on science-fiction could also work.

▼Operetta, opera and musical: *Orpheus in the Underworld* by Offenbach; *Madam Butterfly* by Puccini; *Evita* by Andrew Lloyd Webber and Tim Rice

b. List the main characters and describe them. Can you think of any music which would characterize them? If so, make a note of it. One idea might be to associate each character with a different sort of music—rock jazz, folk, pop, classical—or instrument. Try to limit the number of characters to a hero or heroine, a villain or a group of villains, and one or two comic characters. Also try to bring in minor characters.

c. Write the story you have chosen in not more than five short paragraphs. Each paragraph will be an act. Then sketch out the number of scenes, decide on the number of songs, choose the scenes in which these songs are to be sung, and finally, decide which of the characters is to sing which particular song. Try to fix a tune to each main character, and to each scene. If one is in a disco, for example, you can use disco-music, or, if one is set in a supermarket, you can use soft 'background music'.

d. Include a song at the beginning of the first act which will set the atmosphere of the production, suggest what the opera is about and/or introduce one or two characters. Listen to the opening four minutes of some operas and musicals, such as the ones mentioned in this book. Can you use any of the ideas for your own opera?

e. Now work out how music can best develop the action. Remember that each act should finish with an exciting scene. Listen to some of the act endings in the operas discussed in this book. Can you use any of them—a group of people all singing different words at the same time (like *Figaro*) or the characters leaving the stage completely empty, as they go off in different directions, (like *Carmen* Act Three)? Suggest an opening and an ending for each of your acts. You may find some music which already suits your purpose.

f. Ask your teacher to help you put your musical ideas on paper. Perhaps you can record the tunes. With a bit of luck, you will be able to persuade your friends to perform your opera.